Collin's Chicken Adventures on the Farm

A Children's Learning Guide to Raising Chickens

Written by **Collin Reese Ball**

Edited by **Angela White Ball, PhD**

Collin's Chicken Adventures on the Farm:
A Children's Learning Guide to Raising Chickens
Written by Collin Reese Ball
Edited by Angela White Ball, PhD
Book Layout by Tara Sizemore

Published November 2018
Skippy Creek
Imprint of Jan-Carol Publishing, Inc

ISBN: 978-1-945619-86-1
Library of Congress Control Number: 2018965375

You may contact the publisher:
Jan-Carol Publishing, Inc
PO Box 701
Johnson City, TN 37605
publisher@jancarolpublishing.com
jancarolpublishing.com

This book is dedicated to
my grandparents:
Michael and Carol Ball
and Paige and Susie White

Author's Note

Hello, this is Collin Ball. I love living on a farm. There is so much to do and learn, which is why I am so excited about sharing my farm adventures with you. When my parents agreed to let me raise a few chickens in our backyard, it was the first time I had the responsibility of taking care of my own farm animals. I was also learning how to read in school. My Mommy and I thought it would be fun to take pictures and put my reading and writing skills to use by documenting that first year. I hope you enjoy reading about me and my chickens.

Introduction

My name is Collin Ball. I live on a farm in Russell County, Virginia, which is considered the heart of Southwest Virginia. A ***farm*** is land and the buildings that are used to raise animals or grow crops. ***Agriculture*** is really just a big word for farming because it means the science or practice of raising animals for food, clothing or other products and growing crops.

My family and I raise commercial beef cattle, hair sheep, and American Quarter Horses.

Since I was a baby, I have been helping with the chores on the farm. Here is a picture of me when I was two years old, checking cows with my Daddy.

When I was five years old, I decided I wanted to raise chickens. My Mommy and I decided to write a book to remember my first year raising those chickens and to share my experience with other kids.

Raising Chickens

A chicken is a type of bird that is domesticated. ***Domestic animals*** live in a tame place, like on a farm or in your backyard. Another example of a domestic animal is a horse. Here is a picture of me and my horse Roger at a horse show. Two other words used to describe chickens are ***fowl*** and ***poultry***. Both words mean domesticated birds like chicken, turkeys, and ducks that are kept for eggs or meat.

Chickens are warm-blooded, lay eggs, and are vertebrate. ***Vertebrate*** means that a chicken has a backbone or spinal column. Humans have backbones too. Like all birds, chickens have wings with feathers, but chickens are not good at flying.

There are two main reasons chickens are raised. One is for their eggs and the other is for their flesh or meat, which simply means to make chicken nuggets, chicken sandwiches and all those other tasty chicken dishes. I wanted to raise chickens for their eggs. ***Layers*** are mature female chickens kept for egg production. ***Broilers*** are young chickens raised for their meat. A broiler is usually 9–12 weeks of age when it is processed.

Daddy and I go to farm stores often to buy feed and supplies for the farm. On one of those visits, I saw chicks for sale. A ***chick*** is a baby chicken. It was the spring season, close to the Easter holiday, so the store was full of chicks and all the supplies needed to raise them.

Those chicks were so cute, I wanted to take a few home, but Daddy said, "Not today." On the trip home and almost every day after, I asked my Daddy and Mommy for some chickens. I even had my Daddy help me look up breeds of chickens on my tablet. A ***breed*** is a specific type of chicken. Breeds come in different sizes and colors. I looked at hundreds of pictures of chickens and decided my favorite

breeds had black and white feathers. I really liked the Dominique breed. I will tell you more about this breed later in the book.

After what seemed like weeks and weeks, my Daddy and Mommy told me we were going to an auction at a livestock market in Tennessee to buy some chickens for me. A ***livestock market*** is a large building where farm animals like cows, goats, pigs, and sheep are received and sold to people who bid on the animals. The highest bidder takes the animal home. I was so excited! There were lots of chickens at the livestock market, but my Daddy only bid on two breeds of chickens, the Dominique and Plymouth Rock, because both of these breeds have black and white feathers. We bought two Dominique hens and one Plymouth Rock rooster. This is a picture of the livestock market.

A ***hen*** is a female chicken that is one year or older. Being one year or older means a chicken is an adult. A ***pullet*** is a female chicken under one year of age. A ***rooster*** is a male chicken. An old rooster or ***cock*** is a male chicken over one year of age. A young rooster or ***cockerel*** is a male chicken

under one year of age. Roosters look different than hens. They are bigger, more brightly colored, and usually have a larger comb. This picture shows the physical differences between a rooster and hen of the same breed. The rooster is on the left, and the hen is on the right.

A ***comb*** is the piece of skin on top of a chicken's head, which is commonly red. I think it looks like a Mohawk hair style. The comb acts like the chicken's air conditioner because blood is cooled as it travels through the comb.

My chickens were brought home in wooden crates secured to the back of my Daddy's truck. This is one of those crates.

On the way home, we stopped at a farm store and bought feed, equipment, and supplies to take care of the chickens. These included a coop, feeder, and waterer. A ***coop*** is a house for chickens.

When we arrived back home, it was dark outside, so my Daddy put the chickens in our cattle trailer for the night, where they would be protected. The next morning, as we were getting the chickens out of the trailer and moved into their coop, my

Daddy realized that there might have been a mix-up at the livestock market. Remember, I told you that roosters are bigger than hens, have brighter colors, and a larger comb. Well, one chicken was definitely larger and brighter, but it also seemed that the two smaller chickens, which were supposed to be hens, were roosters too. Three roosters were way too many! My Daddy and I took the two young roosters to a farmer named Mr. Miller, who has lots of chickens. He agreed to let me exchange my two roosters for two hens. It was so nice of Mr. Miller to help me. He also told me how to take care of my chickens.

I named the rooster JB, after my favorite bull rider, JB Mauney. I met JB Mauney in October 2017 at a PBR (Professional Bull Riders) bull riding in Raleigh, North Carolina.

I named my two hens Becky and Cathy, after two of my great-aunts. Here is a picture of my first ***flock***: Becky, JB, and Cathy. A flock is a group of chickens. I have learned it is not easy to take a picture of a flock.

My chickens are ***free-range,*** which means they are allowed to roam freely in the pasture or yard. Every morning, once the sun comes up, I let them out to search for insects and worms to eat. If I do not let them out before going to school, my Pa-Paw will let them out when he comes over to work at the farm.

Chickens are omnivores. ***Omnivores*** will eat both plants and other animals. I am an omnivore (and I bet you are too) because I eat a diet consisting of meat, vegetables, and fruit. My flock loves eating insects, worms, and seeds. Chickens like to eat lots of different things, such as acorns, fruit, grains, slugs, and snails. Like me, my chickens need carbohydrates, protein, and fat. To be sure my chickens get a balanced diet, I provide a pelleted feed using a feeder that is placed in their coop.

The following pictures show the pelleted feed, how I store the feed, and how I fill up the feeder.

Chickens do not have teeth. They have a ***gizzard***, which is similar to a stomach, that contains tiny stones; it helps grind up their food. To help with this digestive process, we buy a bag of oyster shell mix from the farm store and put it in a special container for them. The following pictures show the oyster shell mix and how I fill up the feeder.

I have a water dispenser in the coop, so the chickens have water when inside. I am big enough now to fill the plastic waterer up all by myself, using our water hose. My chickens can also drink out of a concrete water trough that the cows and horses on our farm drink from.

Raising any type of animal is a big responsibility. My Mommy and I make sure the feeders and waterer are filled up. We clean those items frequently. My Daddy lets me use hay he has baled up to keep the nesting boxes in my coop dry and clean. ***Nesting boxes*** are where the hens lay their eggs.

Roosting is when a bird is resting, which, for chickens, is usually at night. My coop has two wooden roosts that my chickens use. It also has a tray that catches the droppings when the chickens are roosting. My Mommy does not like for me to be around the droppings, which is just another word for poop, so she takes care of cleaning this for me. My Daddy and my friend Jerry move my chicken coop to a new location in the yard every week. This ensures that the grass is not killed, the chickens have a clean area to live in, and a fresh supply of worms.

Keeping the coop and equipment clean is important and goes a long way in keeping chickens healthy. Unfortunately, chickens can have bacteria and viruses. They can carry those germs on their feathers, feet, and in their droppings. It is important not to eat or drink where chickens are kept and to always wash your hands with soap and water after petting a chicken or cleaning the coop or equipment. I wash my hands each time I collect eggs.

Every night, the chickens are locked up in their coop to protect them from predators. A ***predator*** is an animal that eats another animal. Chickens have many predators, including foxes, opossums, raccoons, skunks, hawks, and owls. Even cats and dogs can prey on chickens.

Unfortunately, predators attacked my flock. The first time it happened, we got lucky. It was a sunny Saturday afternoon in the summer when my Mommy returned home to find a trail of black and white feathers in our yard. She followed the trail that zig-zagged around our cabin, which abruptly ended at the end of our yard. Mommy would eventually find the two hens, Cathy and Becky. However, JB was nowhere to be found. When Daddy and I got home, we also looked for JB. No luck finding him—alive or dead. After looking at the trail of feathers, my Daddy suspected that a ***raptor***, which is a large predatory bird, had swooped down and taken JB. There are hawks and eagles living on our farm. Everyone was sad. The next morning, my Daddy went to the barn and, to his surprise, found JB in a barn stall. We were so happy! Even JB seemed to be happy. He was missing all his big tail feathers, but had no other injuries. It is a mystery how or why he ended up at the barn. He had never been to the barn before, and it is not close to his coop or the pasture where he would free-range. Daddy and Mommy think that a raptor did take him and perhaps dropped him in flight.

Unfortunately, there was another predator—Mr. Fox. Our next door neighbor, Becky, sent my Daddy a picture of a fox she had seen in her pasture. This is the picture of the fox.

My Mommy had read that the fox is probably one of the greatest threats to chickens. We did not let the chickens free-range for a couple of weeks while my Daddy set a trap for the fox. Time passed and no fox was captured or seen, so Daddy decided to let the chickens go back to free-ranging during the day. Just a few days after this decision, JB did not come in at dusk, which was not like him. The two hens came in without JB, which was also unusual. During her search for JB, Mommy found the fox with JB in his mouth. It was a horrible sight, and JB was dead. Mommy was the most upset because JB was her favorite chicken. I was sad too. This was not the first animal I had lost. Living on a farm, I have seen baby calves born, but I have also seen things pass away. It is the circle of life.

My Daddy set the trap again, and a few days later, we caught Mr. Fox.

After that, I started looking for another rooster. I bought JB #2 and a hen, which I named Annie, after another great-aunt. (If I decide to get a fourth hen, I will probably name her Jamie, after another great-aunt.) JB #2 and Annie are a breed of chicken called Golden Lace Wyandottes.

This is a picture of JB #2.

This is a picture of Annie.

Bringing home a new rooster and hen to live with Becky and Cathy made me understand ***pecking order***. In complicated terms, pecking order is the hierarchy of a group of animals. In simple terms, it means that there is a boss chicken, followed by a second boss, followed by a third boss, and so the pattern continues. Becky and Cathy bully Annie. They even push JB #2 around. I have seen Cathy take a worm out of JB #2's mouth and eat it. Chickens really do have personalities. For instance, Annie is shy. JB #2 likes to think he is in charge and struts his stuff. He crows every morning when he wakes up, usually around 6:30 a.m. Cathy and Becky cluck when you open their coop in the mornings. They also cluck in excitement when their waterer is cleaned and filled up.

My hens lay brown eggs. Roosters do not lay eggs. Hens will lay eggs, even when a rooster is not around. To get chicks, a rooster must be around to fertilize the egg. Chicken eggs can range in color from white to various shades of brown and pale colors. I collect eggs every afternoon. My Grana saves egg cartons that she gets from the grocery store for me to reuse and put my eggs in.

We use eggs to cook with. Fresh brown eggs are delicious! Eggs are a natural source of high-quality protein and also contain 13 vitamins and minerals, including Vitamin D. I also give eggs away or sell them to my neighbor Mr. Bucci and my friends Waylon and Jaylon.

Brown eggs also make the prettiest Easter eggs. This is a picture of me with dyed eggs.

My hens stop laying eggs when they are molting. ***Molting*** is when chickens lose their feathers and regrow new ones. Both hens and roosters go through molting. Molting occurs every year, and in some breeds, twice per year. It can last one to three months. Molting typically occurs when the days get shorter and cooler temperatures arrive. My chickens started molting in mid-October. I do not like when my hens are molting because we have to buy eggs from the store, and I do not think they taste as good. This is a picture of some of the feathers that one of my hens lost when she started molting.

When chickens are not molting, they spend time taking care of their feathers. ***Dust or dirt baths*** are an important part of a chicken's personal hygiene. I am not a fan of taking a bath, but a dust bath sounds like fun. The dust bath helps get rid of parasites on the feathers. ***Parasites*** are tiny animals that live in or on another animal and suck the blood or eat the skin or feathers of that animal. Chicken parasites include mites and lice. Clean feathers are important to a chicken's health. This is a picture of one of the dust bath locations that my chickens use.

A Funny Story

When I first got my chickens, Daddy and I bought some artificial, or fake, eggs and put them in the nesting boxes. These fake eggs are supposed to encourage the hens to lay eggs in the location where they are placed. One day when I was collecting eggs, I mistakenly collected two artificial eggs. I always take the eggs to my Mommy, who makes sure they are fresh, clean, and safe before storing them in the refrigerator. Mommy did not notice that I had brought in the fake eggs. It took her a few days to figure out what we had done.

A Brief Description of Collin's Favorite Breeds

The ***Dominique*** breed is one of the oldest chicken breeds in America. Their feathers are black and white with a striped pattern. Dominiques are raised for their eggs and meat, which means they are dual-purpose. Adults weigh six to eight pounds. Hens lay brown eggs.

The ***Golden Laced Wyandotte*** breed is an American breed. Their feathers are black and gold with a lace pattern. Golden Laced Wyandottes are also dual-purpose. Adults weigh six to eight pounds. Hens lay large brown eggs.

The ***Plymouth Rock*** breed is another American breed. It is a mix of several breeds, including the Dominique. This probably explains why they can come in a variety of colors, including white, blue, buff, and barred. Barred is black and white. The first JB rooster that I bought was black and white. This breed is dual-purpose. Adults weigh seven to nine pounds. Hens lay brown eggs.

Conclusion

I hope you have enjoyed reading about my first year raising chickens as much as I have enjoyed sharing my adventures with you.

Book Vocabulary Words

Agriculture: the science or practice of farming to include raising animals for food, clothing or other products and growing crops

Breed: a specific type of chicken

Broiler: young chicken bred for meat; typically processed at 9–12 weeks of age

Chick: a baby chicken

Comb: piece of skin on top of a chicken's head; usually red in color

Coop: a house for chickens

Domestic Animal: to live in a tame place, like on a farm or in your backyard

Dust Bath: common chicken behavior that consists of bathing with dirt in a shallow depression to get rid of parasites

Farm: area of land and buildings used for raising animals or growing crops

Flock: a group of chickens that are kept together

Fowl: a domesticated bird kept for eggs or flesh

Free-range: chickens kept in natural conditions, allowed to roam freely in the pasture or yard

Gizzard: chicken organ that crushes food with the help of grit such as pebbles or oyster shells

Hen: adult female chicken; one year or older

Layer: mature female chickens kept for egg production

Livestock Market: Building where farm animals like cows, goats, pigs and sheep are received and sold to people who bid on the animals

Molting: shed old feathers to make way for a new growth of feathers

Nesting Boxes: where hens lay eggs in a chicken coop

Omnivores: animal that eats both plants and animals

Parasites: organism that lives in or on another organism (host) and benefits by getting nutrients at the host organism's expense. Chicken parasites include mites and lice

Pecking Order: hierarchy of status for a group of animals

Poultry: domestic fowl, such as chickens, turkeys, ducks and geese; flesh of domestic fowl

Predator: an animal that preys upon (eats) another animal

Raptor: a bird of prey

Rooster: adult male chicken

Old Rooster/Cock: male chicken over 1 year of age

Young Rooster/Cockerel: male chicken under one year of age

Roosting: when a bird is resting or sleeping

Vertebrate: animal with a backbone or spinal column, such as mammals and birds

Reading Comprehension Questions

1. Where is Collin's farm located in Virginia?
2. What is another word for farming that starts with the letter "A"?
3. How old was Collin when he started raising chickens?
4. A chicken is a type of domesticated animal. What is another animal Collin owns that is domesticated?
5. What is the term used for a baby chicken?
6. What state was the livestock market located in where Collin purchased his first chickens?
7. What is one of the two breeds of chicken that Collin bought from the livestock market?
8. What are some of the supplies Collin had to purchase in order to raise chickens?
9. What did Collin's dad notice the next morning after bringing the chickens home from the livestock market?
10. What was the name of the farmer who traded Collin's two young roosters for two hens?
11. What color is a chicken's comb?
12. After what favorite bull rider did Collin name his rooster?

13. Where did Collin get the names for his hens—Becky, Cathy and Annie?
14. What do omnivores eat?
15. Do chickens have teeth?
16. What internal organ do chickens use to grind up their food?
17. What are some of the chores Collin is responsible for in order to raise chickens?
18. What type of predator killed Collin's rooster JB #1?
19. What color eggs do Collin's chickens lay?
20. What does Collin do with all the eggs his hens lay?
21. What is molting?
22. What type of bath do Collin's chickens take?
23. Explain the trick that Collin played on his Mommy when he collected the eggs.
24. What color feathers does the Dominique breed have?
25. What color feathers does the Golden Laced Wyandotte breed have?

Acknowledgments

There are many people to thank for their support with this book. Thank you to: Amy Mize Photography; Bella Mia Images—Michelle Tallada; Lorie Stevens Photography; Emerson Kirby, a friend of my Mommy's, for completing the initial review of the book and sharing contact information for Jan-Carol Publishing, Inc.; and Angela Ball, my Mommy, for documenting my first year raising chickens through pictures and helping me write this book.

About the Author

Collin Ball is a little cowboy from Southwest Virginia. He started "farming" at a young age, riding in his car seat in his Daddy and Pa-Paw's farm trucks to check and feed the cows. Collin loves to be outside riding his four-wheeler or his horse, Roger. He enjoys collecting rocks he finds on the farm and building things on his own workbench in the farm's repair shop. He is a big fan of bull riding and owns some bucking bull stock. In addition, he enjoys playing Little League baseball. When Collin can't be outside, he likes to draw, paint and watch *Scooby-Doo*. Although farming is his first love, Collin loves beach trips where he spends his days collecting shells, searching for sharks' teeth, building sand castles and eating lots of seafood.

Angela White Ball is Collin's mom. She grew up on a beef cattle farm in Southwest Virginia. After completing degrees in agriculture and education at Virginia Tech, she returned to Southwest Virginia to work off the farm. Angela supports her son Collin's many activities. In her free time, she enjoys antiques, the beach, shopping in downtown boutiques and good food.

Angela White Ball and Collin Ball may be reached via e-mail at apwhiteball@gmail.com or on Facebook.

CPSIA information can be obtained
at www.ICGtesting.com
Printed in the USA
LVHW071916161221
706395LV00005B/148